THE GREEK AMERICANS

THE GREEK AMERICANS

Dimitris Monos

CHELSEA HOUSE PUBLISHERS

New York   Philadelphia

Cover Photo: Newsboys in New York City pose by the offices of *Atlantis*, a Greek-American newspaper.

Editor-in-Chief: Nancy Toff
Executive Editor: Remmel T. Nunn
Managing Editor: Karyn Gullen Browne
Copy Chief: Juliann Barbato
Picture Editor: Adrian G. Allen
Art Director: Giannella Garrett
Manufacturing Manager: Gerald Levine

Staff for THE GREEK AMERICANS:
Senior Editor: Sam Tanenhaus
Assistant Editors: Abigail Meisel, Bert Yaeger
Copyeditor: Karen Hammonds
Editorial Assistant: Theodore Keyes
Picture Researcher: PAR/NYC
Designer: Noreen M. Lamb
Layout: Louise Lippin
Production Coordinator: Joseph Romano
Cover Illustration: Paul Biniasz
Banner Design: Hrana L. Janto

Creative Director: Harold Steinberg

3 5 7 9 8 6 4

Library of Congress Cataloging-in-Publication Data

Monos, Dimitris.
   The Greek Americans.

   (The Peoples of North America)
   Bibliography: p.
   Includes index.
   Summary: Discusses the history, culture, and religion of the Greeks, factors encouraging their emigration, and their acceptance as an ethnic group in North America.
   1. Greek Americans—Juvenile literature.
[1. Greek Americans] I. Title. II. Series.
E184.G7M65 1988   304.8′73′0495   87-21833
ISBN 0-87754-880-3
      0-7910-0266-7 (pbk.)

CONTENTS

THE PEOPLES OF NORTH AMERICA

CHELSEA HOUSE PUBLISHERS

A NATION OF NATIONS

Daniel Patrick Moynihan

The Constitution of the United States begins: "We the People of the United States . . ." Yet, as we know, the United States is not made up of a single group of people. It is made up of many peoples. Immigrants from Europe, Asia, Africa, and Central and South America settled in North America seeking a new life filled with opportunities unavailable in their homeland. Coming from many nations, they forged one nation and made it their own. More than 100 years ago, Walt Whitman expressed this perception of America as a melting pot: "Here is not merely a nation, but a teeming Nation of nations."

Although the ingenuity and acts of courage of these immigrants, our ancestors, shaped the North American way of life, we sometimes take their contributions for granted. This fine series, *The Peoples of North America*, examines the experiences and contributions of the immigrants and how these contributions determined the future of the United States and Canada.

Immigrants did not abandon their ethnic traditions when they reached the shores of North America. Each ethnic group had its own customs and traditions, and each brought different experiences, accomplishments, skills, values, styles of dress, and tastes in food that lingered long after its arrival. Yet this profusion of differences created a singularity, or bond, among the immigrants.

The United States and Canada are unusual in this respect. Whereas religious and ethnic differences have sparked intolerance throughout the rest of the world—from the 17th-century religious wars to the 19th-century nationalist movements in Europe to the near extermination of the Jewish people under Nazi Germany— North Americans have struggled to learn how to respect each other's differences and live in harmony.

Millions of immigrants from scores of homelands brought diversity to our continent. In a mass migration, some 12 million immigrants passed through the waiting rooms of New York's Ellis Island; thousands more came to the West Coast. At first, these immigrants were welcomed because labor was needed to meet the demands of the Industrial Age. Soon, however, the new immigrants faced the prejudice of earlier immigrants who saw them as a burden on the economy. Legislation was passed to limit immigration. The Chinese Exclusion Act of 1882 was among the first laws closing the doors to the promise of America. The Japanese were also effectively excluded by this law. In 1924, Congress set immigration quotas on a country-by-country basis.

Such prejudices might have triggered war, as they did in Europe, but North Americans chose negotiation and compromise, instead. This determination to resolve differences peacefully has been the hallmark of the peoples of North America.

The remarkable ability of Americans to live together as one people was seriously threatened by the issue of slavery. It was a symptom of growing intolerance in the world. Thousands of settlers from the British Isles had arrived in the colonies as indentured servants, agreeing to work for a specified number of years on farms or as apprentices in return for passage to America and room and board. When the first Africans arrived in the then-British colonies during the 17th century, some colonists thought that they too should be treated as indentured servants. Eventually, the question of whether the Africans should be viewed as indentured, like the English, or as slaves who could be owned for life, was considered in a Maryland court. The court's calamitous decree held that blacks were slaves bound to lifelong servitude, and so were their children.

America went through a time of moral examination and civil war before it finally freed African slaves and their descendants. The principle that all people are created equal had faced its greatest challenge and survived.

Yet the court ruling that set blacks apart from other races fanned flames of discrimination that burned long after slavery was abolished—and that still flicker today. The concept of racism had existed for centuries in countries throughout the world. For instance, when the Manchus conquered China in the 13th century, they decreed that Chinese and Manchus could not intermarry. To impress their superiority on the conquered Chinese, the Manchus ordered all Chinese men to wear their hair in a long braid called a queue.

By the 19th century, some intellectuals took up the banner of racism, citing Charles Darwin. Darwin's scientific studies hypothesized that highly evolved animals were dominant over other animals. Some advocates of this theory applied it to humans, asserting that certain races were more highly evolved than others and thus were superior.

This philosophy served as the basis for a new form of discrimination, not only against nonwhite people but also against various ethnic groups. Asians faced harsh discrimination and were depicted by popular 19th-century newspaper cartoonists as depraved, degenerate, and deficient in intelligence. When the Irish flooded American cities to escape the famine in Ireland, the cartoonists caricatured the typical "Paddy" (a common term for Irish immigrants) as an apelike creature with jutting jaw and sloping forehead.

By the 20th century, racism and ethnic prejudice had given rise to virulent theories of a Northern European master race. When Adolf Hitler came to power in Germany in 1933, he popularized the notion of Aryan supremacy. "Aryan," a term referring to the Indo-European races, was applied to so-called superior physical characteristics such as blond hair, blue eyes, and delicate facial features. Anyone with darker and heavier features was considered inferior. Buttressed by these theories, the German Nazi state from

1933 to 1945 set out to destroy European Jews, along with Poles, Russians, and other groups considered inferior. It nearly succeeded. Millions of these people were exterminated.

The tragedies brought on by ethnic and racial intolerance throughout the world demonstrate the importance of North America's efforts to create a society free of prejudice and inequality.

A relatively recent example of the New World's desire to resolve ethnic friction nonviolently is the solution the Canadians found to a conflict between two ethnic groups. A long-standing dispute as to whether Canadian culture was properly English or French resurfaced in the mid-1960s, dividing the peoples of the French-speaking Quebec Province from those of the English-speaking provinces. Relations grew tense, then bitter, then violent. The Royal Commission on Bilingualism and Biculturalism was established to study the growing crisis and to propose measures to ease the tensions. As a result of the commission's recommendations, all official documents and statements from the national government's capital at Ottawa are now issued in both French and English, and bilingual education is encouraged.

The year 1980 marked a coming of age for the United States's ethnic heritage. For the first time, the U.S. Census asked people about their ethnic background. Americans chose from more than 100 groups, including French Basque, Spanish Basque, French Canadian, Afro-American, Peruvian, Armenian, Chinese, and Japanese. The ethnic group with the largest response was English (49.6 million). More than 100 million Americans claimed ancestors from the British Isles, which includes England, Ireland, Wales, and Scotland. There were almost as many Germans (49.2 million) as English. The Irish-American population (40.2 million) was third, but the next largest ethnic group, the Afro-Americans, was a distant fourth (21 million). There was a sizable group of French ancestry (13 million), as well as of Italian (12 million). Poles, Dutch, Swedes, Norwegians, and Russians followed. These groups, and other smaller ones, represent the wondrous profusion of ethnic influences in North America.

Canada, too, has learned more about the diversity of its population. Studies conducted during the French/English conflict showed that Canadians were descended from Ukrainians, Germans, Italians, Chinese, Japanese, native Indians, and Eskimos, among others. Canada found it had no ethnic majority, although nearly half of its immigrant population had come from the British Isles. Canada, like the United States, is a land of immigrants for whom mutual tolerance is a matter of reason as well as principle.

The people of North America are the descendants of one of the greatest migrations in history. And that migration is not over. Koreans, Vietnamese, Nicaraguans, Cubans, and many others are heading for the shores of North America in large numbers. This mix of cultures shapes every aspect of our lives. To understand ourselves, we must know something about our diverse ethnic ancestry. Nothing so defines the North American nations as the motto on the Great Seal of the United States: *E Pluribus Unum*—Out of Many, One. ◈

The dome of the Greek-inspired U.S. Capitol was erected in 1857.

THE GREEK INFLUENCE

I f the Greek influence were suddenly erased from America we would find ourselves in a totally alien landscape, one without democracy (Greek for "popular rule"), without universities, without comic and tragic theater. Greece, indeed, created our sense of what it means to be rational, thinking humans, inhabiting a world that can be examined and potentially understood. "The mention of Greece," wrote President James Monroe in 1822, "fills the mind with the utmost exalted sentiments."

He was referring to ancient Greece, not to the Greece of his own era, an oppressed land that had long been subjected to outside invaders and corrupt rulers. Indeed, by the 19th century scarcely any traces of Greece's former glory existed, and it was the United States, crucially influenced by Grecian ideals, that stood on the brink of greatness. By the 1820s, the desire for independence motivated many Greeks to rebel against foreign domination. America's vast natural resources were largely untapped; its robust economy welcomed ambitious newcomers; its political system was free of age-old class antagonisms. American ideals excited the imaginations of distant peoples, including Greeks, many of whom joined the mass exodus of immigrants to the New World.

Exactly how many Greeks crossed the Atlantic is a matter of dispute. According to the U.S. Immigration and Naturalization service, the total number of Greeks who arrived in America between 1820 and 1984 was 692,913. However, this figure excludes immigrants of Greek extraction from Turkey, Romania, Egypt, Cyprus, and other countries. Estimates of the present-day Greek-American population are similarly inexact; they range from about 500,000 to 3 million, depending on the source. Most experts agree the population is about 1.5 million, making it larger than any Greek community outside Greece itself.

Although a few Greeks came to America in the early 1800s, there was no large-scale immigration until late in the century. In the early 20th century, the numbers swelled, peaking between 1911 and 1920. The flood lessened drastically, however, after the Immigration Act of 1924 limited new arrivals from many countries. The influx of Greeks remained low until 1950, primarily because of World War II and the Greek Civil War (1947–1949). In the mid-1950s, Greek immigration rose again, as a result of the Refugee Relief Act, which provided shelter for displaced persons from Italy, Greece, and the Netherlands. It rose for a third time in the late l960s, spurred by the oppressive regime of a military junta and by further reforms in American immigration policy.

Detailed information about the specific sources of Greek immigration is not provided in the United States census, but social scientists maintain that most Greek immigrants came from the southern peninsula of Greece known as the Peloponnesus. The next most numerous group were those who arrived from Macedonia in the north and the islanders from the Aegean and Ionian Seas.

The largest wave of Greek immigrants—the 350,000 who came between 1900 and 1920—were mostly unskilled men from villages on the Peloponnesus. These people usually intended to stay in America no longer than necessary; they hoped to find profitable work, then return home with their savings. Some of them succeeded in this ambition. The generation that came after

In 1925 Greeks arrive at New York's Ellis Island, the chief point of entry for immigrants to the United States.

World War II included more women and professionals, few of whom planned to go back to Greece.

Today Greek Americans inhabit every part of the country, even Alaska, but most remain in the large cities where their immigrant forebears had the easiest time finding steady work. Contemporary Greek Americans have generally blended into the social mainstream, but there are still a few "Greektowns," close-knit communities settled by Greek immigrants in some cities in the mid-Atlantic and midwestern United States.

These immigrants and their offspring have won a secure place in their adopted homeland, but not without a struggle. The first immigrants were rural people, suddenly thrust into exhausting factory work, overcrowded tenements, and the anonymous isolation of urban life.

Such conditions hampered the progress of some Greek immigrants and their offspring, but most entered the mainstream fairly easily. At the same time the group's ethnic identity has been strengthened. For other Americans, the effort to win acceptance has often meant shunting aside memories of the Old World. But Greek Americans remain firmly in touch with their origins. Churches, fraternal organizations, and informal neighborhood gatherings continue to foster community fellowship and pride and continue to tighten the bonds between generations. ≈

A TIMELESS EMPIRE

The mainland of Greece, a mountainous region on the southernmost tip of the Balkan peninsula, lies between three seas: the Aegean to the east, the Ionian to the west, and the Mediterranean to the south. Greece also includes chains of islands. Crete, the largest of these islands, was home to the forerunners of classical Greek civilization, the Minoans, a Bronze Age society formed about 3000 B.C. Like many islanders, the Minoans—or Cretans—were avid sailors. They frequently set out from their rocky coastline and explored the surrounding Mediterranean waters. Their voyages acquainted them with two other thriving peoples, the Hittites and the Egyptians, who became their trading partners.

Back home, the Greek civilization flourished under King Minos. In Knossos, the ancient Minoan capital, the Minoans built a stone palace. Artisans covered its walls with frescoed sea images of fish and blue dolphins, symbols of the Minoans' mastery of the Aegean Sea. Ingenious workmen fitted palatial bedrooms with adjoining private bathrooms, each supplied with fresh rainwater channeled through clay pipes. Other talented Minoans modeled beautiful clay pots, pounded metal into decorative and useful tools, and carved delicate

Minoans filled their homes and temples with such mythological images as that of the snake goddess, portrayed here in an ancient statuette.

figurines out of ivory. According to one historian of this glorious era, the court at Knossos "lived in a refined luxury hardly to be paralleled west of China."

Constructed during the Bronze Age—before 2000 B.C.— Knossos was twice toppled by geological upheavals, apparently earthquakes. The Minoans rebuilt it after two such disasters, but another cataclysm in about 1400 B.C. left their city and the palace hopelessly shattered. Archaeologists have uncovered much of the palace's skeleton, reconstructing its design and finding ample evidence of the rich Minoan culture and its language. According to some historians, at about the same time as the earthquakes occurred, Crete suffered an invasion by Mycenae, a city on mainland Greece that had dominated the peninsular Peloponnesus since the 17th century B.C. but had been checked in its seaward expansion by the powerful Minoans.

In 1400 B.C., with Knossos defeated, Mycenaean fleets at last freely sailed the Mediterranean in pursuit of commerce. Their expeditions led them to the opulent coastal cities of Asia Minor, which were prized for their proximity to the Black Sea and its trade routes. In approximately 1200 B.C., the Mycenaean general Agamemnon headed an invasion of one such city, Troy. This resulted in a series of sieges.

A 7th-century B.C. vase depicts the Trojan horse, inside of which Greek soldiers supposedly hid before launching a surprise attack on the city of Troy.

*The allegorical figure
Democracy crowns the people of
Athens in a relief from 336 B.C.*

After several years of conflict the Mycenaeans prevailed. By 1100 B.C., another Greek people, the Dorians, swept into the region, took Peloponnesus, chased the Mycenaeans northward, and fanned out over parts of Asia Minor (present-day Turkey). Much as the conflict itself mattered to the Greeks, posterity remembers it chiefly because it inspired two epic poems, The *Iliad* and the *Odyssey*, composed and recited by the poet Homer in the 8th or 9th century B.C. Some experts claim these epics were composed as early as the 10th century B.C., before the Greeks had evolved an alphabet. Along with the Old Testament, produced at about the same time, Homer's works form the cornerstones of Western literature. Indeed, the *Iliad* is often called the world's greatest poem. It chronicles the last year of hostilities between the Greeks and the Trojans, focusing on the tragic story of Achilles, a noble warrior who agrees to join the battle only after his best friend is felled by an enemy spear. The *Odyssey*, composed after the *Iliad*, recounts the journeys and homecoming of another Greek warrior, Odysseus, after the conclusion of combat in Troy.

Like many works of the imagination, Homer's epics rest on a solid bedrock of fact. Indeed, their geographical details are so reliable that the 19th-century archaeologist, Heinrich Schliemann, used the *Iliad* and the *Odyssey* as guides when he excavated the site of ancient Troy, located in present-day Turkey.

Growth and Expansion

Although Homer created poetry of the Mycenaean age, he himself belonged to a later period of Greek history inaugurated about 500 years after the Trojan War. Like their Bronze Age forebears, the Greeks of the 6th through 8th centuries were sailors whose immense curiosity led them to travel widely and gather information about the world around them. Seeking relief from overpopulation and political turmoil, they migrated across southern Europe. By the 7th century B.C., Greek cities had cropped up throughout the Aegean and Ionian islands and in Asia Minor. Continuing westward across the Mediterranean, Greeks settled in Spain, France, the lower half of Italy (known in Latin as *Magna Graecia*, or Great Greece), and the large island of Sicily, which lies just off the "toe" of boot-shaped Italy. Today thriving Sicilian cities such as Syracuse and Agrigento contain the splendid ruins of ancient Greek palaces and temples.

Greek metropolises sprang up not only abroad, but also on the mainland. Because the terrain was moun-

Since the Renaissance, many artists have been inspired by classical subjects, such as The Death of Socrates, *painted by Jacques Louis David in the 1780s.*

tainous, these newly formed settlements developed in isolation from one another and thus evolved into fiercely independent, self-governing city-states, each with its own commerce and colonies. They produced wine, olive oil, linen, and pottery, and exchanged them abroad for grain, lumber, and slaves. As the economies of these regions expanded, their system of government evolved. In most cities, the leadership of kings—who had dominated the Bronze Age of the Minoans and Mycenaeans—gradually gave way to the rule of a few aristocratic land owners and wealthy traders. Greek city-states established a pattern for many European societies in the centuries to come.

Athenian Democracy

The most innovative Greek city-state was Athens. It was there, in 594 B.C., that the ruler Solon (the "lawgiver") established history's first democratic government by granting legal rights and a voice in civic matters to local farmers and tradesmen. One of early Greek civilization's "Seven Wisemen," he established Athenian society and divided it into four classes, each with its own specific role in the city-state. His brilliant experiment was continued by another Athenian statesman, Cleisthenes, and by the early 6th century B.C., democracy was flourishing. This is not to say that everyone supported the new government. The egalitarian arrangement did not please all Athenians. The aristocrats, in particular, were enraged at having to cede some of

The Parthenon was designed by two 5th-century Athenian architects, Ictinus and Callicrates.

their power to mere farmers and even enlisted the aid of Sparta, a rival city, in their attempts to dislodge democracy. Still, the "rule of many" prevailed.

Athenian democracy made all free men (but not women and slaves) independent citizens rather than passive subjects ruled by an all-powerful king. Each citizen participated in political debates and elections and openly voiced his opinions in public. This freedom of expression infused all aspects of Athenian society and the arts as well as politics. The added stimulus of contact with foreign cultures, provided by Athens's bustling ports, spawned perhaps the greatest cultural boom in the history of Western civilization.

During the 5th century B.C., philosophers and artists reigned supreme in Athens. The playwrights Aeschylus, Sophocles, and Euripides created lyric plays so magnificent that they set the foundations for tragic theater and remain unimpeachable models for today's drama. No less admired were the comedies of Aristophanes, which satirized public figures in daring, witty, and ingenious language. In *The Clouds* (423 B.C.), Aristophanes poked fun at his contemporary, the philosopher Socrates, said to be the wisest man in Athens. Socrates dedicated his life to enlightening his fellow Athenians by quizzing them tirelessly about moral and political matters, never shrinking from posing embarrassing or dangerous questions. Socrates probed so deeply that a tribunal charged him with corrupting the youth of Athens and sentenced him to death in 399 B.C.

Fortunately, his teachings were preserved by his disciple Plato, whose written versions of Socrates' dialogues laid down a main plank in Western philosophy. Plato was himself a teacher of mathematics and philosophy and founded a school in Athens, the Academy, where he taught until his death in 347 B.C. His many works, including the *Crito* and *The Apology*, examined issues such as the absolute nature of right and wrong. His most famous dialogue, *The Republic*, speculates on

the qualities of the ideal state, a topic at the heart of Athenian life.

In addition to establishing the roots of Western philosophy and literature, ancient Greece was the birthplace of modern architecture. No public endeavor engaged Athenians more than sacred structures built in the 5th century B.C. atop the Acropolis, a hill of sheer

Draped female figures, known as caryatids, support the entablature of the Erechtheum, an Acropolis temple honoring the mythological god-king of Athens.

The Discobolus (Discus Thrower), a bronze masterwork by the 5th-century sculptor Myron, survives only in a Roman, marble copy.

rock where Athens was based until the 6th century B.C. Most of the structures survive only in fragments, except for the Parthenon, a sacred temple offered to the city's patron, Athena, the goddess of wisdom. The Parthenon surpassed all the other temples in its grandeur. Today, it is well preserved, and its symmetrical lines embody the essence of the classical Greek style that has been copied so often in later times. These buildings were designed by Athens's finest architects and constructed by hundreds of stonecutters, artisans, and sculptors. Each was handpicked by the statesman Pericles, a patron of the arts, diplomat, and warrior who governed the Athenian democracy for 30 years after coming to power in 461 B.C. When Pericles ordered construction of the Parthenon in 447 B.C., he regarded the project as an homage both to Athena and to the glory of the city. Remarkable as the results are, they pale beside Pericles' grandest accomplishment, molding Athens's Golden Age in an era torn by war.

War Between the City-States

From 499 B.C. to 388 B.C, the Athenians were twice at war. First, they sparred with the Persian empire for control of Greek-founded cities in Asia Minor. Allied with Greek settlers in Asia Minor and its fierce rival Sparta, the Athenians waged a 51-year war against the mighty and much more numerous Persians. In 448 B.C., the Persians were decisively beaten by the Athenians, who had become the economic and political giants of the Aegean and the region's greatest sea power.

Athens's new prosperity was eyed jealously by its former ally Sparta. Unlike the Athenians, the martial Spartans obeyed a rigid code of constant vigilance, self-discipline, and physical courage that left no time for artistic pursuits. They despised the Athenians' mercantile ambitions but coveted their dominion at sea and their prosperous colonies in Asia Minor. Further pressure to go to war stemmed from the conflict between the pro-Spartan league and the league favoring democracy. Hostilities between the two cities steadily intensified and in 431 B.C. erupted in the Peloponnesian War, a conflict that raged desperately for 27 years and destroyed the Athenian empire. This titanic struggle between these two very different Greek cultures is the

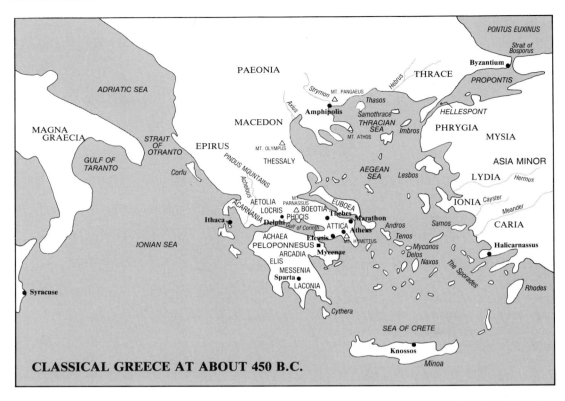

CLASSICAL GREECE AT ABOUT 450 B.C.

subject of an eight-volume study by Athenian historian Thucydides.

Athens lost control over the Greek world, but its legend and accomplishments persisted. The grand culture of Pericles' era was proudly adopted by many Greeks as their own. And although ancient Greece had never been a unified nation, its people shared a common identity as Hellenes (supposed descendants of the mythical figure Helen, daughter of the god Zeus). They were also strengthened by a common regard for the teachings of Socrates and Plato and by their love of the works of Homer and the great playwrights. Athens no longer commanded a maritime fleet or an empire. It reigned for centuries, however, over the imagination (and culture) of the West.

The Hellenistic Period

Today we refer collectively to the land occupied by these independent enclaves as Greece, but the land's inhabitants historically referred to it as Hellas, after Hellen, son of Deucalion. Thus the epoch presided over by Athens was termed "Hellenic." And the great period to follow was the "Hellenistic." Its seeds were planted by the next ruler of the Aegean world, Philip II of the northern Greek country of Macedon, who came to power in 359 B.C. and brought classic—or Hellenic—culture to his court. He even summoned Aristotle, the most famous student of the Athenian philosopher Plato, whose impact on science and philosophy was to prove enormous. For three years Aristotle tutored Philip's son Alexander, training him to be a model prince.

After Philip's death, Alexander acceded to the throne in 336 B.C., at the age of 20, and within 6 years realized his father's ambition of invading and conquering the vast Persian empire. Calling himself "Alexander the Great" and patterning his life on that of Achilles, the hero of the *Iliad*, Alexander's deepest allegiances were to Athenian culture rather than to the Macedonian state.

As Alexander marched eastward, he built or left his mark on more than 60 cities, naming 15 of them after himself. The most splendid of these was the Egyptian city of Alexandria, a magnet for Hellenistic scholars. The mathematician Euclid, and the astronomer and geographer Eratosthenes, among others, journeyed to Alexandria, the Athens of the Middle East, and were given access to a library containing more than 500,000 volumes.

Once again, Hellenic culture outlasted an empire. This time it was Alexander's that fell. By 31 B.C., Egypt, the last of his spectacular kingdoms, had succumbed to the next great rulers of the West, the Romans. They absorbed the Hellenistic world into their own empire, signaling the end of Greek independence.

Athens, however, remained a center of education and philosophical inquiry. Thus, although the Romans had conquered Athens, the Greek city-state's intellectual brilliance captivated them.

The Advent of Christianity

The Romans modeled their civilization after that of ancient Greece during the first three centuries of Roman rule. But in the early A.D. 300s, a momentous change swept through the Roman empire. According to legend, the emperor Constantine was preparing to enter battle in A.D. 313, when he saw a flaming crucifix in the sky bearing the words "In this sign thou shalt conquer." Constantine took this as a divine message and he adopted the religion of Christianity, then just 300 years old and practiced only by a small minority whom the Romans persecuted. After his own conversion, the emperor sought to protect Christians by issuing the Edict of Milan, allowing the free practice of the faith.

By A.D. 330, Constantine had changed not only his religion but also the seat of his empire. He forsook Rome, the ancient capital, for the city of Byzantium, which he renamed Constantinople (today's Istanbul), on the Bosporus Sea in Asia Minor. A center of art and

A relief shows Spartan troops seizing an Athenian colony in Asia Minor during the Peloponnesian War.

Alexander the Great charges into battle against the Persians in this Byzantine mosaic.

philosophy, it was also birthplace of an independent branch of Christianity, which became known as the Eastern Orthodox church.

A rivalry heated up between Rome and Constantinople and the versions of Christianity they represented. Today, because the Roman Catholic and Eastern Orthodox churches differ from the most recent branch of Christianity, Protestantism, the two ancient sects seem similar. And indeed, even in Constantine's day, they bore a marked resemblance. Both believed that the holy communion was *ex opere operato*, a direct conferral of God's grace, and both venerated the Virgin Mary, the mother of Christ. However, these similarities were outweighed by crucial differences. Members of the Eastern Orthodox church, for example, rejected the authority of the Vatican in Rome, obeying instead the leadership of the patriarchy, an office established under Constantine. The two religions also evolved dissimilar rites. Eastern Orthodox Christians sang their mass instead of speaking it, did not celebrate the mass daily, and received the Eucharist—or the sacrament of Communion—from a spoon, rather than by hand.

These points of divergence created a schism, or division, between the two churches in the 400s. This split widened irreparably in 1054 when Pope Leo IX for-

MT.
PARNASSUS

MODERN GREECE

mally condemned the head of the Orthodox church of Constantinople. The conflict heightened in 1204, during the Fourth Crusade, which was originally undertaken as a united attempt by both Christian churches to wrest control of Palestine from the Muslims. But Roman Catholic forces stationed in Constantinople coveted its great riches and stormed the city walls, seizing control of the capital.

Henceforth, the Roman Catholic church ruled over a vast empire that extended to the mainland of Greece. Already weakened by earlier invasions launched by Slavs and by people from the neighboring Baltic lands, Greece was no match for fresh assaults from French and Italian forces. Genoa, Venice, Pisa, and Normandy all carved out parts of the ancient civilization. By the 13th century, its glories were only a memory as foreigners occupied a land inhabited chiefly by impoverished peasants.

Ottoman Rule

As badly as the Greeks suffered at the hands of other Western European nations, they fared worse under their next conquerors from the East, the Ottoman Turks. In 1453 these terrifying warriors captured Constantinople and thus absorbed the territories of Byzantium and Greece. Neither Roman Catholic nor Eastern Orthodox, the Ottomans were Muslims. Like Jews and Christians, the Muslims were monotheists, or believers in one god. They worshiped Allah and viewed all Christians as infidels, dangerous nonbelievers. Bent on undermining the religious and governmental authority of the Eastern Orthodox church, the Turks committed many indignities against it, such as auctioning off top ecclesiastical posts to the highest bidder.

Outraged by this treatment, some Greeks abandoned their homeland, fleeing to different corners of

The Byzantine emperor Justinian built the Church of the Hagia Sophia (Holy Wisdom) between the years A.D. 532 and 537 in Constantinople, today the Turkish city of Istanbul.

Europe—Hungary, Poland, Germany, France, Holland, Austria, and Russia. Many intellectuals and merchants settled in Italy, particularly in Venice, Livorno, and Naples. Suddenly infused with Greek culture, these cities kept alive its ancient traditions of philosophic and scientific inquiry and helped stimulate the 15th-century rediscovery of classical civilization that was so much a part of the Renaissance.

Not all Greeks chose to leave their native country, however. Those who remained endured the rule of the Ottomans until 1821, when, at last, they united against the Turks to gain their national freedom. The majority of these insurgents, peasants and seamen, lacked provisions and weapons, yet they managed to keep the mighty Turkish empire on the defensive. By 1823, news of their success spread across the continent and donations poured in from sympathizers in other countries, particularly in Great Britain.

In 1821 the Hellenic insurgents suffered a severe setback when Russian support was not forthcoming. But in 1827, the insurgents received direct military support when a fleet of combined French, British, and Russian naval vessels entered the war on behalf of the independence movement. Two years later, the defeated Turks signed the Treaty of Adrianople, granting freedom to the Greeks, but leaving them with only a fraction of the land that was rightfully theirs. The Ionian islands and Crete still remained in foreign hands. Not until 1913 did Greece regain control of these territories.

Domestic Troubles

Even as their warships steamed into the Mediterranean Sea to reinforce the Greek nationalist movement, England, France, and Russia had an ulterior motive—extending their own influence over the land. Toward this end they installed a Greek-born diplomat, Joannes Antonius Capodistrias—formerly an adviser to Russia's Czar Alexander I—as governor of Greece. He proved

enormously unpopular, however, and was slain by assassins in 1831, only to be replaced by an equally inept leader, Otto I, a Bavarian prince.

These political setbacks were matched by a series of economic misfortunes. In the late 19th century the country's traditional exports, silk and olives, gave way to currants, sold in vast quantities to French vintners whose vineyards had been devastated by plague. When France recovered, the bottom fell out of the market for Greek-grown currants, destabilizing an already fragile economy. Meanwhile the country's population swelled and its limited supply of arable land yielded too little to feed a growing population.

Destitute farmers fled family plots to seek employment in cities, but few could compete with the numbers of skilled workers used to satisfy the demands of the urban job market. In consequence, Greek peasants realized that their best chances for survival lay not in Greece, but in a land thousands of miles away. By the 1890s, villagers were journeying en masse to the port towns of Patras and Piraeus, points of embarkation for the unknown: the shores of North America. ❧

At the turn of the century emigrants embark from the Greek city of Patras for the United States.

A Greek woman peddles vinegar from house to house in the Peloponnesian village of Kynouria.

IMMIGRATION

Long before the first waves of immigrants began to arrive from Greece, some of its sons played a part in the Hellenic peopling of North America. The spirit of experimentation and exploration weathered the turmoil of subsequent ages, and Greeks took part in navigating the expanding geography of the known world. Johan Griego, for instance, a Greek who lived in Genoa, Italy, belonged to the crew that sailed with Christopher Columbus in 1492. Griego thus became the first Greek to set foot on North American soil. Thirty-five years later, a seaman named Theodoros joined a Spanish expedition that explored the Gulf of Mexico and the coasts of Florida. Juan de Fuca, born Apostolo Valeriano on the island of Cephalonia, signed on with an expedition, also Spanish, that explored the Pacific Coast. De Fuca discovered a strait, now named after him, which contains the boundary line dividing Canada from the United States.

More than two centuries later, when the American colonies asserted their independence from England, their cause was aided by some early Greek immigrants, including John Paradise, a scholar of ancient Greek who was a friend of Benjamin Franklin's and a protégé of Thomas Jefferson. Paradise married the daughter of one of Virginia's first families, and their house, the

Samuel Gridley Howe, an American supporter of Greece's war for independence, poses in Greek military garb.

Ludwell Paradise House, was the first colonial residence restored in Williamsburg, Virginia.

Émigrés and Philhellenes

In the 1820s, as Greece rebelled against the Ottoman Empire, a small number of Greek refugees and orphans arrived in the United States. They were welcomed here because Greek insurgency was championed in America, especially in New England, which, as the new nation's cultural center, felt a strong attachment to the legacy of ancient Greece. Relief committees organized in the United States found contributors among leading Americans. And the struggle was vociferously defended by public figures such as John Quincy Adams, who later served as the sixth president of the United States (1825–1829); Daniel Webster, the New Hampshire Congressman celebrated for his eloquent orations; Josiah Quincy, the Massachusetts politician who served as president of Harvard University; renowned educational reformer and first president of Antioch College, Horace Mann; and Edward Everett, publisher of the influential *North American Review*.

More dramatic and direct support for Greece came from the "philhellenes," or lovers of Greece. Three New Englanders, Lieutenant General George Jarvis, Colonel Jonathan P. Miller, and Dr. Samuel Gridley Howe, formed the "Yankee" contingent that sailed to the Mediterranean to put their lives on the line for Greek independence. These volunteers advanced the Greek cause in America by lauding the character of the Greek people in letters and reports sent from the front or composed following the heat of battle. A few of these adventurous Yankees even adopted Greek war orphans and arranged passage for others to America.

An outstanding American philhellene was the humanitarian Dr. Samuel Gridley Howe. Born into a distinguished Boston family in 1801, Howe graduated from Harvard Medical School. He foiled his family's expectations by deciding not to practice medicine in his hometown, choosing instead to join the Greek uprising. He arrived in Nauplia, Greece, in January 1825 and stayed in the country for six years, serving as a medical officer, soldier, and as an architect of hospitals. In order to win American support for the Greek struggle he wrote the *Historical Sketch of the Greek Revolution.* In it he praised the Greek people for possessing intelligence, industriousness, and hospitality.

Upon his return to the United States in 1831, Howe assumed the directorship of the Perkins Institution, (formerly the New England Asylum for the Blind), the foremost such organization in the world. But Greece beckoned again, and in 1866 he returned to chair the American Relief Committee in support of Crete, which had started its own insurrection against the Turks. During this second trip, Howe met Michael Anagnos, who eventually became the doctor's son-in-law as well as one of the world's chief authorities on the education of the blind and deaf.

In 1822, the Greek island of Chios, situated in the Aegean Sea, was invaded by the Turkish fleet. Thousands of Greeks were massacred and many children orphaned. One of them was 6-year-old George Musalas Colvocoresses, who watched as his uncle was murdered and his grandmother fatally beaten. George's father, who had escaped to the Austrian consulate, managed to rescue the rest of the family and sent George to the United States, entrusting him to Howe's care. Raised in New England, Colvocoresses enrolled in the military academy at West Point and became a captain in the United States Navy. His son, George Partridge Colvocoresses, also pursued a naval career and retired with the rank of rear admiral after 45 years of active service.

Another of the many Greek orphans brought to America by Dr. Howe was John Celivergeos Zachos, whose friends eventually included the poet William Cullen Bryant, the journalist Charles Anderson Dana, and other leading writers of 19th-century New

The Ottoman slaughter of Greek civilians in 1822 fired the imagination of French painter Eugene Delacroix, who began work on The Massacre of Chios *that very year.*

England. Zachos himself was an eminent scholar, teacher, and one of the first Americans to demonstrate that blacks, then often regarded by whites as members of an inferior race, were fully capable of being educated.

A third Greek orphan child reared in New England, Lucas Miltiades, owed his success to Colonel J. P. Miller, an American philhellene who fought during the 1821 war for Greek independence. After a particularly bloody battle, Colonel Miller found and protected a child whose father, a captain in the Greek revolutionary army, had been killed by the Turks only a few months after his wife's death. Colonel Miller described his first encounter with the boy:

> While walking the streets, I observed a boy and a girl, hand in hand, almost naked. The girl appeared about 9 and the boy about 7 years of age. On inquiry, I found that they were orphans, and that their father . . . had nobly fallen in battle. This boy I have taken as my own with the consent of the government, and by the blessing of God who early taught me to feel the loss of a father, I am determined that in me he shall find a friend and protector.

Refugees from Asia Minor seek shelter in the stable of a Turkish inn on their way home to Greece.

Brought to the United States by Colonel Miller, Lucas Miltiades adopted his protector's last name. He attended school in Vermont, studied law, and settled in the territory of Wisconsin, where he was elected a member of Congress in 1891, the first Greek American to attain such high political office. (The fate of Miltiades' sister is unknown.)

The Greeks who arrived in the United States before the 19th century made little effort to retain their ethnic identity. Yet because many had developed unusually successful careers during the 1800s, they were able to help foster a positive image of Greece and of Greek identity in the minds of other Americans.

During the late 19th century, Greek peasants—such as this shepherd—were reduced to poverty by the country's corrupt aristocracy.

The Classical Style

Among the late-18th- and early-19th-century developments that helped raise the American estimation of the Greeks entering the United States was the fashionable interest in ancient Greek culture, especially its architecture. Designers and builders in the United States began to imitate ancient Greek models. Partly inspired by archaeological excavations in Greece, the style caught on in American cities, especially during the 1820s and 1830s.

A famous example of the so-called Greek Revival style is the Second Bank of the United States, built in Philadelphia, Pennsylvania, in 1824. Its designer was William Strickland, who modeled the bank's exterior after the Parthenon, which exemplifies the design known as the *amphiprostyle* temple. Strickland received support from Nicholas Biddle, a major patron of the style who pursued it further in his hometown of Andalusia, Pennsylvania. In 1833 Biddle commissioned his architect, Thomas Walter, to create a majestic Doric façade to cover an existing structure. (Architecture in Doric mode, such as the Parthenon, unites massiveness with simplicity. Columns, or shafts, are mounted on a stylobate, or base, that supports the topmost structure, or entablature.) Walter's use of Grecian columns, executed in wood, influenced many subsequent architectural façades. Walter designed other buildings in Greek Revival style, most notably the wings for the U.S. Capitol building in 1865. The dome of the Capitol, also designed by Walter, was the first of many distortions of the style imitated by state capital buildings that were constructed around the nation.

The Peak Years

In the late 1800s, Greece was once more beset by political unrest and economic decline. Victory in the War of Independence had brought the country freedom, but the governments that succeeded Ottoman rule scarcely improved on it. A corrupt and indifferent ruling class ignored the plight of the peasants, who suffered dire economic setbacks, including the currant crisis of 1890.

Worse, an oppressive system of taxation required individual peasants to pay from 10 to 40 percent of their income to the government, whereas small businesses contributed only 5 percent and the ruling elite surren-

In 1921 these Greek women immigrated to America in order to join their prospective grooms.

dered nothing. One Greek official succinctly summarized Hellenic society of that time by dividing it into two classes: those who, through honest labor, replenished the public coffers; and those who, through mismanagement, depleted them. Disheartened peasants contemplated emigrating to America. Luckily, the Greek government enacted no policy limiting emigration, even as encouraging news filtered back from those who had chanced life in the New World and met with some success.

One typical anecdote of this period illustrates how naive the peasants were about the riches available across the Atlantic. According to this story, a shepherd from Greece who had recently landed in New York City was met by a cousin already living there. As they walked the city streets, the newcomer spied a gold coin lying on the pavement. He picked it up, studied it closely, then tossed it into the gutter, much to the surprise of his American cousin, who demanded an explanation. The newcomer replied that after his long voyage he was too tired to pick up coins and preferred to wait until the next day. Then he would gather as many as he

By 1920 Greek Americans in Chicago operated more than 10,000 small businesses, including the meat market pictured here.

wished—everyone knew that in America the streets were paved with them.

To counter these misconceptions, the Greek government, fearful of losing able-bodied men in the event of war with Turkey, spread hair-raising stories about life in America. As difficult as life had become in Greece, an outflow of human resources could not be allowed to continue. Newspapers published—and probably fabricated—letters from disillusioned immigrants in the New World pleading with their compatriots to remain in Greece. But the exodus of Greeks to the vast continent across the ocean did not abate.

Most of those who left between 1899 and 1910 were men seeking better economic prospects or escaping Greece's compulsory military service. Some of the immigrants, however, were single women hoping to find husbands whose expectations did not include a dowry, a custom—practiced in Greece and elswhere—whereby women handed over to their husbands a sum of money as part of the marriage arrangement. The task of raising the dowry fell to fathers and brothers, and the financial strain on poor families could be unbearable, especially in times of widespread economic hardship. The most significant level of emigration from Greece occurred during a 25-year-period that commenced in 1900. Not only had markets for Greek currants dried up during the 1890s, but production was badly damaged at the turn of the century. It seemed that little but financial misery could be expected in the Old World.

Not all immigrants wanted to sever their ancestral ties. Many men went to the North American continent hoping to earn money they could send to their families back in Greece. They had not severed their ties with the homeland and they were determined to alleviate their country's economic troubles.

Shepherds, farmers, tradespeople, and fishermen set out for North America from rural villages in Greece. As a group, these immigrants were barely literate, the most educated among them having received only two or three years of schooling. Practically none spoke English. A smaller percentage of immigrants, about 8 to 10 percent, arrived from Asia, central Europe, and North Africa, where immigrant Greek populations had been living for centuries. They tended to be better educated and financially better off than those departing from Greece.

Although most immigrants from Greece had grown up on or near farms and were ideally suited for rural occupations, they usually had such painful recollections of failed crops and hungry mouths that they wanted nothing more to do with agriculture. Upon arriving in America, they either stayed in New York City or congregated in other cities where industrial jobs were plentiful. Chicago was a popular destination, as were smaller New England cities such as Lowell, Massachusetts, home to many textile and shoe factories. Some adventurous newcomers headed to the western frontier, to Nevada, Utah, and California, taking jobs in the mines and on construction crews laying tracks for the Pacific spur of the transcontinental railroad.

Even those immigrants who disdained heavy labor were forced into menial jobs because they did not speak English. Some of the earliest arrivals peddled cigars, flowers, or candy from pushcarts; others became bootblacks or dishwashers. When fluctuations in the American economy put street vendors out of work, they flocked to industry. (During the 1870s and mid-1890s, for example, after the trauma of the American Civil War, the tremendous economic growth that resulted during the Reconstruction was interrupted by unemployment, bankruptcies, and bank failures. Workers saw jobs and wages slashed; unrest and strikes became prevalent.) Greeks began working alongside immigrants from other nations in slaughterhouses and tanneries. Often they earned less than their fellow laborers, sometimes as little as $4 a week, but at least jobs were available, especially after bosses observed the dependability and stalwartness of immigrant laborers from Greece.

Although the U.S. economy was buffeted by periods of decline, American industry and American railroads were expanding at an unprecedented rate, creating vast new sources of employment. This expansion drew increasing numbers of people from around the world to the United States's shores. A work system developed among many immigrant groups, including Greeks, called the *padrone*, or boss, system, which aided greenhorns fresh from the Old World. For a percentage of the immigrant's salary, a padrone helped newcomers find work and housing and often acted as an interpreter and go-between. Many of these bosses acted honorably, and seriously tried to help their compatriots. Others abused the power they wielded over newly arrived immigrants for whom life in their adopted country could be bewildering.

The shoeshine business was particularly notorious for its greedy padroni, who paid immigrants' boat fares, started them out with pocket money, then virtually enslaved them. Bootblacks were often required to put in 15-hour days, without Saturday or even Sunday off. In most cases their bosses took a portion, if not all, of their tips. A year's worth of tips, totaling as much as $100–$200, sometimes exceeded the bootblack's income during that time. The contract, expected to last a year, sometimes was stretched out much longer. Some

Factories such as this Massachusetts textile mill, photographed c.1915, welcomed Greek laborers.

shoeshine boys remained under the padrone's thumb for years; the cannier immigrants broke free at the first available opportunity. Eventually, federal legislation and the efforts of organized labor led to the downfall of the padrone system.

These conditions bolstered the intention of many immigrants to go back to Greece as soon as they had saved enough money to return to their homeland, the country of their birth and the place where they hoped to live out their days. To these early newcomers America was a temporary way station, a means of escaping the grip of poverty.

Despite these abuses, Greeks welcomed the opportunity to send their sons abroad, misled by false reports of generous padroni whose guidance would spur young workers toward success in America. Parents were sometimes deceived by their own motives. So eager were they to receive the money their sons would be sending home to Greece that they chose to think only the best of America and its manifold opportunities. In reality, however, America proved to be a hard and demanding place. Rather than finding a surfeit of riches, immigrants discovered the toil and sweat that was propelling the United States into the forefront of industrialized nations. For many immigrants from Greece, the notion of returning to their families and homeland with pockets full of new wealth was no longer tenable. The harsh conditions of the workplace, combined with the opportunity to build a new life in the United States, stiffened the resolve of Greeks to remain in the New World.

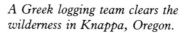
A Greek logging team clears the wilderness in Knappa, Oregon.

LIFE IN AMERICA

In the mid-19th century, when large-scale immigration to the United States began, most immigrants came primarily from Germany, Ireland, Norway, and Sweden, countries whose inhabitants readily blended into the American mainstream. Fair-skinned and usually Protestant, these newcomers were relatively successful at winning acceptance from their American-born neighbors, who in many ways scarcely differed from them. German and Scandinavian immigrants further deflected potential animosity by settling in the Midwest and Pacific Northwest, sparsely populated areas with little job competition and ample room for settlers willing to clear their own land for farming. Those who chose to live in cities and enter the industrial workplace usually had a rougher time of it. The Irish, for example, met resistance from native-born Americans, generally in the form of anti-Catholicism. But Irish immigrants, at least, had the advantage of speaking English.

In the late 19th and early 20th centuries, immigration patterns began to shift. A growing supply of newcomers came from southern and eastern Europe, many fugitives from depressed economies or oppressive governments. At this time Greeks began to leave their homeland in force, often headed to the United States. In 1848, only one Greek came to our shores, compared

49

with 19,061 Irish and 51,593 Germans. Between 1900 and 1910, however, more than 167,000 Greeks departed from their native land, approximately one-quarter to one-fifth of the country's entire labor force. And the majority of those immigrants headed for the United States.

As the sources of immigration shifted from northern Europe and the British Isles to central, eastern, and southern Europe, many native-born Americans received their first glimpse of cultural features that to them seemed exotic. A high percentage of newcomers, for example, practiced religions such as Judaism or Orthodox Christianity. In addition, many of these immigrants spoke languages bereft of audible similarities to English, unlike German and most of the Scandinavian tongues. A final difference was that, by and large, these latest arrivals congregated in northeastern cities already inhabited by the children and grandchildren of immigrant groups gaining their first foothold in their new homeland. These more established immigrant groups were unprepared for the onslaught of newcomers who drove down wages and also threatened the ethnic makeup of provincial neighborhoods.

In 1909 John Masourides slew a policeman in Omaha, Nebraska, and touched off a violent anti-Greek riot.

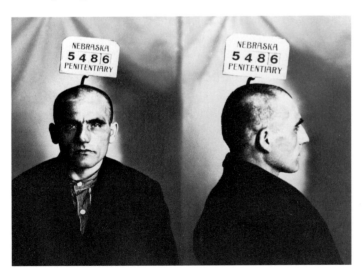

Like scores of immigrants before them, many Greeks found jobs working on railroads in the American West.

In short, antiforeign sentiment was afoot not only among long-established Americans but also among those on the way to becoming Americanized. This sentiment received ugly encouragement from notorious "experts" on ethnicity who promulgated ludicrous theories warning against America's "mongrelization" by different ethnic groups. Eugenics, a pseudoscientific theory that held certain races to be superior to others, was on the rise.

Bigotry

One English word that Greek immigrants could have picked up easily enough originated in their own language: *xenophobia*, fear of strangers or aliens. It defines an attitude that some Greek newcomers encountered after they arrived in America. In a few communities where Greek immigrants had become a noticeable presence incidents of open prejudice flared up. Rhode Island, for example, was home to a sizable population of Greek immigrants who made a living by fishing off the Atlantic coast. They became the target of a bill brought before the state legislature in 1909. It attempted to ban all noncitizens from fishing for lobsters. In Lowell,

An employee of the Corcoris sponge empire with a day's catch in Tarpon Springs, Florida, c.1920.

Massachusetts, where Greeks at one time made up more than a third of the population, workers employed chiefly in local textile mills were harassed by Irish Americans and French Americans, who resented the favoritism shown hardworking newcomers from Greece.

Greeks faced violent resistance in several states in the American West, including California, Utah, and Colorado. The most publicized display of anti-Greek sentiment occurred in Omaha, Nebraska, in 1909. The incident began on February 19, when a Greek immigrant killed a policeman during an argument. Several days later a meeting was held to discuss ways of ridding the community of its 1,200 Greek-American residents. Stirred by emotion, the peaceable gathering turned hostile, then violent, until the crowd went on a rampage through the Greek district of Omaha. When the melée subsided, the entire Greek community had been burned to the ground and its inhabitants had been driven out. Greeks hoping to settle in Mountain View, Idaho, were confronted by a mob of masked men, who descended on the town and demanded that the immigrants clear out within 24 hours.

Sometimes immigrants unwittingly brought about antiforeign sentiment through their own actions. During a strike at a Chicago diesel shop in 1904, Greek immigrants, unaware of the circumstances behind the strike and, at the same time, eager to enter the job market, gladly agreed to take the strikers' jobs, thus breaking the strike. The strikers were enraged, as were the entire organized labor movement and its supporters in the press. Even other Greeks rebuked the workers for jeopardizing the status of the community at large.

Getting Ahead

Despite widespread prejudice, Greek immigrants saw opportunity in America. For many, employment in its factories, mines, and as street vendors was the first step toward a more promising career. Once they accumulated enough capital, ambitious Greek Americans opened their own small businesses. Fruit stands, flower shops, confectioneries, and, especially, restaurants became the province of Greek-born entrepreneurs. Often they were family run, with the entire household pitching in.

A unique example of this entrepreneurial spirit emerged in Tarpon Springs, Florida, a small community on the Gulf of Mexico. The Florida coast, like that of Greece, was rich in sponges. Therefore, in 1905 John Cocoris and his brothers—Greeks who had settled in America—brought to the United States 500 sponge divers from the Aegean and Dodecanese islands in Greece. Cocoris provided these immigrants with an opportunity to ply their unique skill. Soon the brothers dominated the entire U.S. sponge industry and Tarpon Springs developed into a prosperous Greek-American enclave. In 1940, 73 percent of the town's 3,400 inhabitants were of Greek descent.

Today Greek-American grocers still cater to the Mediterranean tastes of their customers.

The Cocorises represented a trend among Greek immigrants anxious to graduate beyond backbreaking physical labor and low hourly wages. After a few years or months in America, most of them started their own small businesses. The first generation born in America followed their example. Most of the Greek-American children had begun their working lives as bootblacks or peddlers and in this way served valuable apprenticeships in commerce.

The Greek-American talent for entrepreneurship was not lost on their neighbors. As early as 1909, a study of Chicago's Greektown stated the matter in terms that reflect the crude generalizations commonly used at the time, even in scholarly papers: "During the short time he has been in Chicago the Greek has estab-

The Zenos Brothers Confectionary Store, pictured here in 1916, catered to the citizens of Port Arthur, Texas.

lished his reputation as a shrewd businessman. On Halsted Street they are already saying, 'It takes a Greek to beat a Jew.' "

During the years preceding World War II, Greek Americans achieved their greatest success as owners of small businesses. This phenomenon was especially prominent in New York City and Chicago. For example, in 1908, although Chicago's Greek-American population was below 20,000, the group held a virtual monopoly on sweet shops, owning 237 confectioneries. By 1913 they owned several hundred lunchrooms and restaurants in this mecca for central and southern Europeans. The situation was similar in New York. In Manhattan alone, fewer than 20,000 Greek Americans owned 151 bootblack parlors, 113 fruit shops, 107 lunchrooms and restaurants, 70 confectioneries, 62 retail fruit stores, and 11 wholesale produce dealerships.

Neighborhood Life

By 1930, when immigration to the United States had been reduced drastically, Greek Americans were found mostly in New York, Illinois, Massachusetts, Pennsylvania, and California. Today, the situation is much the same: The cities with the largest Greek populations are New York, Chicago, San Francisco, Boston, and Lowell, Massachusetts. The Greek population is highest today in the northeastern United States.

Most immigrants who came to the United States from Greece had been impoverished sheep herders, farmers tilling tiny plots, fishermen, and artisans such as cobblers and tinsmiths struggling to subsist. Raised in villages, they sought to recapture rural neighborliness as they established close-knit Greektowns in America's bustling cities.

One notable Greek-American community is Astoria, a neighborhood in New York City's borough of Queens. Detroit's Greektown, filled with restaurants and cafés, is one of the city's most popular areas. In many other

Greek Americans in Oregon gather for the groundbreaking ceremony of the Holy Trinity Church.

cities, Greek Americans operate small businesses, especially restaurants and coffee shops, which now are fixtures of the urban landscape. Greek, or Eastern Orthodox churches, with their rounded domes and distinctive crosses, adorn almost every American city.

Food and entertainment reminiscent of native Greek cuisine and culture can be found in the Greek-American *tavernas* of our large cities and in the autumn bazaars and festivals often held on the grounds of the local Greek Orthodox church. These joyous occasions strongly resemble the jubilant atmosphere of a Greek village during religious or national holidays, when the central square is turned into a marketplace where merchants hawk their wares, magicians perform their tricks, food vendors tempt the nose and palate, and the people dance continuously to live music until late at night.

Among the hundreds of visitors to the yearly festivals of the Greek-American communities, one can see many Americans brought there by their Greek friends, the music, the dancing, and interest in becoming acquainted with another element of the American mosaic.

Another place where many Americans have had occasion to sample Greek culture is in a Greek restaurant. Even in the smallest towns, many restaurants are owned by Greek families. Diners, luncheonettes, and pizza parlors have introduced Americans to *souvlaki* and *gyro* sandwiches made of chunks of lamb or beef, tomatoes, onions, yogurt, and garlic sauce, all wrapped in a flat bread called *pita* and usually accompanied by a Greek

At a Chicago lamb roast, Greek Americans raise their glasses in a toast.

Greek coffeehouses, such as this one in Utah, served as community centers for newly arrived male immigrants.

country salad containing lettuce, tomatoes, onions, *feta* cheese (made from goat's or sheep's milk), and anchovies.

Greek cuisine is one of the richest, most varied, and most original in the world. Many dishes are international favorites, including *dolmathakia* (mince or rice balls wrapped in grape leaves), *domates yemistes me rizi* (baked tomatoes stuffed with rice), and *souvlakia* (shish kebab). Many Greek dishes are served with piquant sauces made with such ingredients as butter, olive oil,

tomato juice, lemon juice, eggs, pot herbs, and spices.

Arni tes souvlas or roast lamb on a spit, is the national Greek dish; it is believed to date back to Homer's time. Another popular lamb dish, *frikasse*, consists of lamb stewed with lettuce, onions, anise, parsley, and butter, and served with a sauce made of eggs and lemon. An unusual lamb dish is *kokoretsi*, roasted pieces of liver, heart, and other internal parts. Another popular dish is *stifatho*, a stew made with beef, onions, olive oil, vinegar, tomato juice, and pepper.

Coffeehouses

In the late 19th and early 20th century, Greek-American communities often gathered in the local *kaffeneion*, or coffeehouse. Typically, it was an inexpensive enterprise: A store was rented, tables and chairs were installed (for conversation and card playing) and the walls were covered with maps of Greece and portraits of Greek heroes. The establishment usually bore a familiar name such as "Acropolis" or "Parthenon." Coffee was brewed in a back kitchen, then served by the proprietor himself, along with baked pastries such as *phyllo*, a delicate, flaky, paper-thin dough baked in sheet form.

In this comfortable environment, immigrants of all classes, professionals and laborers, congregated, finding companionship, exchanging gossip and news. For newcomers, coffeehouses were especially valuable as refuges from the bewildering foreignness of America's teeming cities. In these bustling establishments, the new arrivals could find advice, leads and offers for jobs, and hous-

In 1921 Meletios Metaxakis, founder of the Greek Orthodox Archdiocese of North and South America, visited with eminent members of Chicago's Greek community.

ing. In *The Greeks in the United States*, Theodore Saloutos describes the atmosphere of the typical coffeehouse in the late 19th century:

A Greek Orthodox nun instructs young congregants in their religious heritage.

> The air . . . was choked with clouds of smoke rising from cigarettes, pipes, and cigars. Through the haze one could see the dim figures of card players or hear the stentorian voices of would-be statesmen discussing every subject under the sun. No topic was beyond them. European problems were resolved readily, and all were at their peak when the politics of Greece were discussed. On the marble-top tables one could see diagrams of Near Eastern division, military strategies, and imaginary advances or retreats. . . . When the subject under discussion was not politics, it was the weather, the stock market, the faults of others, the capabilities or limitations of the community priest and teacher, life in the hereafter and what language departed souls spoke, and the possibilities of a Greek becoming president of the United States. . . . On visitors, especially those not understanding Greek, such discussions could have an almost terrifying effect; they could easily have been mistaken for quarrels. But they were all verbal; no blows were delivered. . . .

In New York Greek Americans annually parade in celebration of their homeland's Independence Day.

In large Greek-American communities, such as Lowell, Massachusetts, coffeehouses also provided live entertainment—solo musicians, small combos, silent film screenings, floor shows, even strong-man exhibitions. A unique form of entertainment was a kind of charade enacted by a *karagiozopechtis*, or silhouette performer, who made rapid hand gestures and voice modulations while standing behind a backlit white sheet. The drama often centered on Greece's war of independence against Turkey, with the performer playing the parts of both sides. At the turn of the century, there were half a dozen silhouette performers in the United States and they appeared in coffeehouses throughout the country.

Another, but less wholesome, form of entertainment was gambling. Owners and patrons sometimes were fined and coffeehouses were raided by police. In Chicago, illegal gambling got so out of hand that the mayor closed down the city's coffeehouses, which he classified with dance halls and opium dens as breeding grounds for vice. Still, such activities were the exception, and not the rule. Perhaps it was all the more unfortunate for the immigrants themselves because they had little money to start with. Betting involved small stakes; these were not tournaments for highrollers. Nevertheless, the high-pitched public outcry led community groups, civic leaders, and newspaper editors to clean up the environment of coffeehouses. Young men were then advised to steer clear of these establishments.

The Church

The furor and scandal caused by the coffeehouses contrasted starkly with the overall sedateness of Greek-American community life, which revolved around the church. Indeed, Greek Americans were often more devoted to their religion than to their ethnic roots. And churches commonly played an important role in preserving the culture of the homeland. When between 300 and 400 Greek immigrants settled in an area, one of their first collective actions was to organize a Greek Orthodox community with a president of the parish, a secretary, a treasurer, and various church committees. More affluent communities permanently employed a priest; the less affluent ones hired a clergyman for Sunday mass and for important religious holidays. Usually, religious services were celebrated in hired halls or in church buildings loaned to them for special occasions by Protestant congregations.

As soon as a Greek community was well established, its members purchased an existing church and used it until they could afford to buy a tract of land and build their own place of worship. The favored architectural style was Byzantine—patterned after the decorative art that enriched Byzantium, the seat of the Eastern Orthodox Church.

Originally, the motive behind establishing churches in America was purely religious. However, recent immigrants, separated from Greece and alienated from American institutions, have expanded the role of the church, transforming it into the community's unifying cultural institution. In addition to serving its religious function, the church also houses Sunday schools, Greek afternoon schools, and charitable societies. It also accommodates social activities such as dances and lectures. In brief, the church in the United States has evolved into the cultural center for Greek-born people of both sexes, all ages, and all economic and social standings.

More so than with Protestant and Catholic parishes, Orthodox parishioners tend to acquire an intimate knowledge of one another that spills over into life outside the chapel. The priest, who frequently appeals to more successful parishioners on behalf of the unemployed or recent arrivals from Greece, is well acquainted with the entire community. This intimacy prevails even though contemporary Greek parishes have swelled to many times their original size.

The elaborate Orthodox service includes priests in ornate vestments, hymns sung by priests, chanters, and choir, rituals involving icons, or sacred images, gifts of bread following the close of the service, and sugared wheat to memorialize dead parishioners. This ceremoniousness heightens during Easter week, when a symbolic tomb of Jesus is carried three times around the inside of the church while the congregation intones solemn dirges. On the night of Great Saturday, even the comparatively undevout attend religious services. On this occasion, the church remains dark and silent until midnight, when the priest lights the candles of worshipers who, in turn, light those of their neighbors. Everyone then celebrates the resurrection of Christ in song and carries the candles to their homes, trying to keep them lit the entire way. If they succeed, their residence is considered blessed for the following year.

Celebrations and Social Clubs

Apart from church events, there are other community activities that ritually honor important events in Greek history. The most notable of these is March 25, the date on which the Greeks declared their independence from the Turkish Ottoman Empire in 1821, a proud event in recent Greek history that is commemorated by

(continued on page 73)

AGES OF
TRADITION

MAXIMIANVS

The 6th-century emperor Justinian I, shown (above, center) with his courtiers, was a staunch defender of the Greek Christian doctrine that emerged during the Byzantine Empire. St. Appollinaris adorns a Byzantine church in Ravenna, Italy (below); the facing portrait of the infant Jesus and the Virgin Mary is in a Yugoslavian monastery.

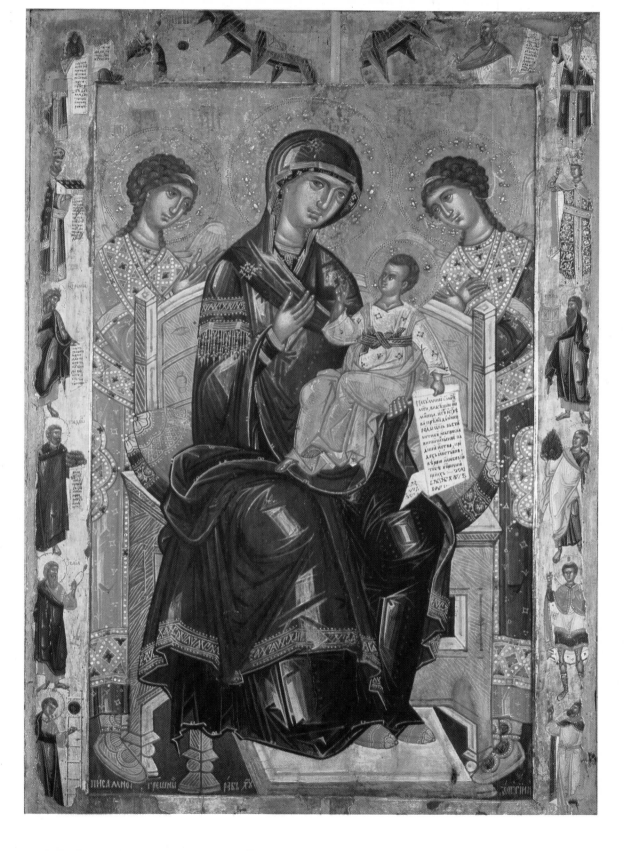

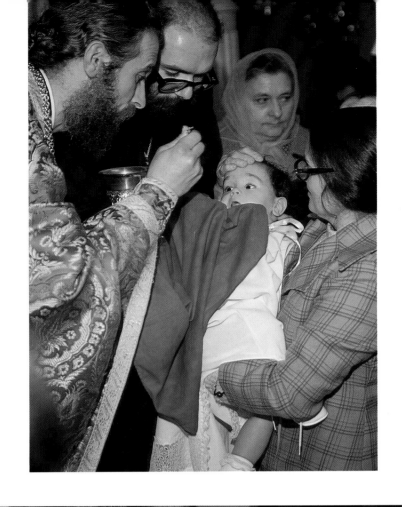

At an Eastern Orthodox church in Astoria, New York, a priest serves Holy Communion to both the very young and the very old. Although assimilation has become a reality for many Greek Americans, religious devotion remains a bulwark of ethnic identity.

Eastern Orthodox celebrations on Good Friday and Easter include a procession with a box made of flowers—symbolizing Christ's tomb—and a candle-lighting ceremony. On less solemn occasions, Greek Americans enjoy parties that feature souvlaki *and elaborate pastries.*

Because no substantial wave of Greek immigrants has arrived in North America since the early 1900's, Greek-American neighborhoods have gradually lost some of their distinctiveness. Where they persist, more than a glimmer of the Old World is visible.

(continued from page 64)

Greek Americans. In many cities every year, thousands of Greek Americans, some dressed in traditional costumes, parade through the main streets and place a wreath at an important local monument, such as the Liberty Bell in Philadelphia. Speeches are made to commemorate the independence struggle of 1821 against Ottoman domination and to celebrate the freedom that life in the United States and Canada affords. The day usually ends with a dance performed by local Greek folk dancers.

The first Greek immigrants originally came to the United States hoping first to find work that paid well, and then, after amassing enough money, to return to the homeland with the money they made. The worldwide Great Depression of the 1930s, however, made immigrants realize that it might be years before they could return to Greece and to their native towns or villages. With this realization came a nostalgia for the old country that led to the formation of many national organizations, which gathered together the natives of a particular Greek region, island, or town. Today there are more than 60 such fraternal organizations in the United States, representing all the major regions of Greece, such as Macedonia, Thrace, and Sparta, and even more out-of-the-way places, such as the islands of Ikaria and Chios.

In 1910 the executive council of the Hellenic League for the Molding of Young Men—a Chicago-based group—sits for a group photograph.

Before many of the Greek immigrants arrived, Greek scholars and students founded cultural and intellectual societies in the United States. One of the first was the Plato Society, organized in Boston by several Greek scholars. Nearby Cambridge was the home of Helicon, the first university club in the United States, founded at Harvard University in 1911 by a group of Greek scholars and students. The original goals of Helicon were to promote intellectual and social cooperation among its members, to give moral support and financial assistance to worthy students of Greek descent, and to foster an appreciation for modern Greek culture among other people. Today, Greek university clubs with similar goals can be found in most of the larger American cities.

One of the most recent organizations established by Greek Americans for newcomers from the homeland is the Hellenic American Neighborhood Action Committee (HANAC), established in 1972. The *1986 Yearbook of the Greek Orthodox Archdiocese of America* lists 63 different Hellenic-American federations and organizations established to help Greek immigrants adjust and protect the rights of Greek Americans. These groups can be divided into two major categories, national and local.

The national organizations have chapters in localities with sizable Greek populations. Some serve no spe-

Greek bakers in New York City prepare traditional pastries.

cific purpose and function mainly as centers for the Greek-American community. Some are benevolent organizations. Their membership is open to all Greeks in the United States. Other general organizations, such as the American Hellenic Educational Progressive Association (AHEPA), emphasize traditional customs and also the importance of civic responsibility. Others stress the preservation of Greek linguistic and cultural identity in America, such as the Greek American Progressive Association (GAPA). Others serve to unite people whose ancestors came from a specific region of Greece. Still others are specialized, educational, artistic, or professional organizations such as the Modern Greek Studies Association (MGSA).

Established in 1922 in Atlanta, Georgia, AHEPA is one of the oldest and most influential of these national fraternal organizations. AHEPA sponsors the celebration of Greek Independence Day on March 25, perpetuates the Greek language, and assists Greek Americans in their efforts at assimilation. The organization requires its members to be legal citizens of the United States and woos influential Americans from all backgrounds to join. Invitations have been accepted by a number of United States presidents, senators, congressmen, and other national and local political leaders.

Large urban centers also support societies that focus on specific aspects of Greek culture, such as music and folk dancing. Dancing is a favorite form of entertainment among Greek Americans, and Greek fraternal organizations compete to hold the most successful and elaborate dance of the year. Because there are many such organizations in major American cities, a dance of some kind takes place almost every two weeks. One of the best-known dancing troupes is Theseus, founded in Philadelphia. Theseus has performed at Carnegie Hall in New York, the Kennedy Center for the Performing Arts in Washington, and in many other places. ✎

In 1943 a steelworker in Pennsylvania relaxes with a Greek-language newspaper at a local diner.

FITTING IN

The role played by Greece in 20th-century history has generally helped the status of Greek Americans. During both World War I and II, Greece sided with the United States and its allies. In 1950, Greek combat troops were included in the United Nations military forces that battled the armies of communist North Korea and the People's Republic of China. Two years later, Greece joined the North Atlantic Treaty Organization (NATO), founded in 1947—Western Europe's military and strategic counterpoint to the Warsaw Pact of Eastern European nations and the Soviet Union. Because of the traditionally friendly relations between their country of origin and their adopted land, Greek Americans—unlike German Americans, Japanese Americans, and Russian Americans—have been spared accusations of having dual loyalty or of being more loyal to the nation from which they emigrated than to the United States.

Greek-American Values

Prejudice often has less to do with the alliances—or misalliances—among governments or whether certain nations have been foes in war, than with irrational objections to different skin colors or ways of speaking. Again, Greek Americans have done well on this score. Despite the hostility some Greek Americans encountered in the early 20th century, color and racial origin

A Greek soldier poses in the traditional military costume of his homeland c.1900.

have not presented an insuperable barrier to the relatively fair-skinned Greeks.

Greek Americans also profit from their long history of rapid assimilation. Centuries of foreign conquest by Rome, Venice, England, Italy, and Turkey schooled Greeks in the art of adjusting to—and absorbing—alien cultures. This capability served them well in the United States. Although approximately 80 percent of Greek immigrants came from rural backgrounds, where most were farmers or artisans, nearly all of them settled in urban areas and successfully adjusted to the job markets there.

Another vital factor in the adjustment of immigrants is the compatibility between their own values and those that define American middle-class society. Like many other Americans, those of Greek extraction emphasize the importance of individual achievement and self-reliance. Resourcefulness, pride, social commitment—all these classically American values trace back to an earlier time and place: ancient Greece.

These similarities intrigued a number of scholars who studied the Greek-American community shortly after immigrants began arriving in substantial numbers. In 1913, the American scholar Thomas Burgess described Greek immigrants as conservative, family-oriented, enterprising, and morally strict. Because fellow Americans shared these values, Burgess argued, newcomers from Greece would easily fit into their adopted homeland. Burgess believed further that Greek Americans would improve the moral standard of American society, which he felt was speeding toward decline. "The Greeks," he wrote, "are not corrupting us; we are corrupting them." Other notable Americans shared his views, including the trial lawyer Clarence Darrow, best known for his work in civil liberties. He once cautioned: "See that you Hellenize the Americans rather than Americanize the Greeks."

At about the same time that Burgess wrote his study, other commentators also addressed Greek immigrants and their values. Most predicted success for the group in the United States. In 1911, the social scientist Henry Pratt Fairchild pointed to a strong resemblance between the ancient Greek character and the modern, and found the latter persisted in the contemporary habits of adventurousness, resourcefulness, courtesy, politeness, self-confidence, and hospitality. Fairchild also admired the Greeks' patriotism and temperance. In 1909, another sociologist, Grace Abbott, judged the early Greek immigrants to be largely ignorant of American customs and language. Yet she also found them to be enterprising, hard-working, and family-oriented—a sure bet to prosper in the New World.

Much of this praise for Greek Americans was based on observations of their family life. Traditionally, the Greeks viewed the family in highly practical terms. Men chose brides according to family reputation, social standing, and wealth, and women relied on their families to find proper matches. Children often received a great deal of attention and affection from their parents. Perhaps for this reason, grandparents often live in Greek-American households.

Early in this century, Greek-American Elias Varessis established the Garden Fruit Store in San Antonio, Texas.

During the early years of immigration, Greeks usually preferred to marry within their own community. But because there were very few Greek women in the United States, men sometimes returned to Greece and brought back brides from their home villages. This was more common among those Greeks who did not intend to invest a lifetime in America. Yet even those planning to stay on looked for wives in Greece, rather than contend with American women, whose comparative independence distressed them. They frequently took such independence as a sign of loose morality. In 1926, it was estimated that only one in five Greeks in this country entered a mixed marriage. In the 1960s, the number had grown to 3 out of 10. By the mid-1970s the figure reached approximately half. Today, even those who have married outside the Greek community express admiration for Greek couples, and praise the virtues of a Greek marriage. Because the family has remained a vital and cherished institution to Greek Americans, and because it is the chief preserver of Greek ideals and the Greek way of life, marriage between Greeks seems likely to ensure the survival of a distinct ethnic group in the United States.

A Changing People

Greek Americans have tended to adopt the prevailing values of their neighbors. For example, separation and divorce, practically unheard of within the Greek immigrant community, have gradually made inroads into the population. This change is most dramatic among Greek-American women born in the United States or Canada.

Another characteristic American trait, competitive striving for success, surfaced among the first wave of Greek immigrants. In Greece, social and economic opportunities were sharply limited. Few citizens expected to rise above the station to which they were born. However, a ticket to America was considered a passport to quick riches and success. It was unthinkable to receive so grand an opportunity, not capitalize on it, and be forced to return to Greece a failure.

Greek immigrants felt trapped into succeeding and, as a result, many did. So did their offspring and later immigrants. The 1980 U.S. Census indicates that Greek immigrants as a group are among the least formally educated ethnic groups in the country, yet their income exceeds the average for all other ethnic groups by 10 percent and falls only 4 percent below the average for the total American population. Other studies have shown that compared to other ethnic groups, Greek Americans have lower unemployment rates and fewer of them live in poverty. An unusually high percentage own their own businesses. Even those who work for others generally climb into managerial positions. A recent study showed that in certain areas—Boston, for instance—no Greeks lacked jobs or depended on welfare.

Because of their limited education, few of the first generation of Greek Americans entered professions such as law and medicine. By 1950, however, the population's presence in these professions had increased almost fivefold and could be found in professional positions 36 percent more frequently than other Americans. This trend has continued. A great number of second-generation Greek Americans are professionals, including managers and administrators. The overall income of Greek Americans rises with each generation.

The Spoken and Written Word

For non-English-speaking ethnic groups, learning and using the English language is the essential first step toward assimilation. But the early Greek immigrants wanted to keep alive their own ancient language. Toward this end, only Greek was spoken at home, in church, and in afternoon schools established specifically to perpetuate the Greek language. Thus many Greek-American children learned to speak Greek before they learned English. At the same time, they often lagged

behind their peers in the public school classroom and had to contend with teasing and taunting by their playmates.

Their difficulty managing English sometimes erupted into a resentment against their own language compounded by their parents' insistence that they attend classes in Greek while other children were free to play. Out of necessity, the children of the early Greek immigrants diligently set about learning English and helping their parents over the language hurdle.

The competitive, ambitious Greek immigrants eventually realized that English was an indispensable tool to success. A milestone was reached in 1971 when the Greek church recommended a translation of church liturgy into English. Today, both languages are used in

Staff members of the Atlantis, *a Greek-language newspaper, are photographed in action c.1950.*

the sermons and in parts of the Eastern Orthodox mass.

The written word was also crucial to new immigrants' adjustment to America. Numerous newspapers, pamphlets, books, and humor magazines in Greek were available to the immigrant community. As early as 1911, a study of Greeks in the United States doubted "if there is another foreign nationality . . . that publishes so many newspapers in its own language in proportion to its total population as the Greeks." Although many of these publications were short-lived, they

Greek Americans helped the U.S. government during World War I by purchasing liberty bonds in great quantity.

served the Greek-American community—and its newcomers, in particular—by acting as a bridge to English-speaking society.

Neos Kosmos (*New World*), the first Greek newspaper in America, appeared in Boston in 1892 but ceased publication eight years later. The second paper, *Atlantis*, was founded in New York City in 1894 and did not publish its last issue until the middle of the 1970s. In 1910, there were at least 16 Greek newspapers in America. The daily *Ethnikos Kyrix* (*National Herald*) made its appearance in New York City in 1915 and has been in circulation ever since. The Greek papers eventually began publishing books and pamphlets aimed to provide the recent immigrant with much-needed information. More recently, the Greek-American press has concentrated mainly on the concerns of Greeks in the United States. This position has enhanced the adjustment of Greeks in America.

The Greek-language press has usually urged immigrants to participate directly in American life. A campaign during World War I led Greek Americans to purchase an estimated $10 million in Liberty Bonds by May 1918, thus helping the U.S. and the Allies to defeat Germany. Chicago's Greek-American community alone spent more than $2 million, averaging $167.83 per capita, the highest average of any ethnic group. ॐ

MAKING AN IMPACT

For many years, even after ethnic minorities were accepted as a valuable part of the American landscape, they were locked out of important areas of our society such as politics and finance. As a result, ambitious immigrants and their offspring usually channeled their energies into fields where merit alone was rewarded. Greek Americans are no exception to this pattern; the most distinguished members of the group made their mark in education, the sciences, the arts, and commerce.

Teaching and Healing

Michael Anagnostopoulos (1837–1906), or Anagnos, as he was known in America, was born in a mountain village in Epiros, the northwest region of Greece. After graduating from the National University of Athens, he worked as editor in chief for the *Ethophylax* (*National Guard*), one of the first daily newspapers in Athens, until he met Dr. Samuel Gridley Howe, who persuaded him to come to the United States. Upon his arrival in Boston, Anagnos became a teacher of Latin and Greek at the Perkins Institute for the Blind in Boston, run by Howe. After Howe's death, Anagnos took over the directorship of the institute and met with even more success than his mentor. Indeed, Anagnos was eventually

Michael Anagnostopoulos—who shortened his name to Anagnos— devoted his life to educating the deaf and blind.

recognized as the world's foremost educator of the deaf and blind. His pupil Helen Keller became a writer despite being blind, deaf, and mute.

Anagnos's influence also reached many other Greek Americans. In 1891, 10 years before the first Greek parish was established in Boston, Anagnos helped found the Plato Society, one of the first Greek educational institutions in America. He then cofounded three more Greek intellectual societies in Boston: the Mutual Help Society, *Verenthi*, and *Vasarras*.

By the late 1890s, the small Greek-American community in Boston felt a strong need for organization. Anagnos, a constant visitor at its restaurants and coffeehouses, organized a fund for the creation of a Greek church. Once the Greek community was organized, he became its first president. Five years later, he was a founder of the National Union of Greeks, the first national Greek organization in America. He also served as its first president.

Anagnos and other Greek-American intellectuals in New England shone as examples not only for future generations of Greek Americans but also for members of other ethnic groups. As Bishop Charles Laurence of Boston wrote:

> We are receiving from Eastern Europe thousands, upon thousands of people. We are wondering, sometimes with dread, what their influence will be in our American civilization. Granted that the mass of them have not in them the qualities of the Greek, Anagnos; nevertheless, the fact that he has lived here and done his work gives us hope and confidence . . . .

Dr. George Papanicolaou's Pap smear has saved the lives of thousands of women by enabling doctors to detect at a very early stage malignancies of the cervix and uterus.

The lives of millions of women around the world are saved every year thanks to the work of Dr. George Nicholas Papanicolaou, a Greek-born scientist who migrated to the United States. Papanicolaou was born in 1908 in the small town of Kyme on the island of Evoia and received his medical degree from the University of Athens in 1904. He pursued further studies at the German universities of Jena, Freiburg, and Munich. In 1913, he came to the United States with his wife, and a year later joined the faculty of the Cornell Medical College in New York City, becoming Professor of Clinical Anatomy in 1924.

In 1928, Dr. Papanicolaou presented the results of years of research in a paper entitled "New Cancer Diagnosis," describing a technique he had developed to diagnose cancer, particularly cancer of the female reproductive system. More than 15 years passed before Papanicolaou's results were accepted by the medical community. By the 1940s, the Papanicolaou test (or Pap smear) was used as a routine screening technique throughout the world. This development was followed by a sharp reduction in the death rate from cancer of the uterus and the cervix. Papanicolaou's work is considered among the most important ever made in the field of cancer research and detection. In November 1961 he became the director of the Miami Cancer Institute, renamed the Papanicolaou Cancer Research Institute after his death three months later. An indefatigable worker, Papanicolaou was rumored never to have taken a vacation.

The tradition of excellence in education and science that began with Anagnostopoulos and Papanicolaou has been continued by more recent Greek immigrants and their American-born children. The 1985 *Who's Who in America* indicates that science and education are the fields in which Americans of Greek origin excel most frequently. Dr. George Kotzias (1918–1977), a Greek-born neurologist, pioneered the treatment of Parkinson's disease. Dr. Peter Diamandopoulos (born on the island of Crete in 1928) served as chairman of the Department of Philosophy and dean of the faculty at Brandeis University, president of Sonoma State University in California, and then president of Adelphi University on Long Island. Dr. Matina Souretis Horner (born in Boston in 1939) is president of Radcliffe College. Peter Liacouras (born in 1931) is president of Temple University in Philadelphia. John Brademas (born in 1927) graduated from Harvard University and became a Rhodes Scholar, receiving a doctorate from Oxford University. He worked as a professor for one year, then was elected to Congress, representing Indiana in the House of Representatives and serving in the U.S. capital until 1980. He has been awarded several honorary doctorates from various universities, and in 1981 was named president of New York University, the nation's largest private institution of higher learning.

The Arts

The glorious tradition of Greek art has found new expression in the modern medium of film and in ancient ones such as music, theater, and the plastic arts. The first important Greek artist to work in America was Constantino Brumidi, who was born in Rome in 1805 to a Greek father and an Italian mother. Brumidi's gifts were so evident that at age 13 he gained admittance to the Academy of Fine Arts. Eventually, he gained the favor of Pope Pius IX, whose portrait he painted. Along with two other artists, Brumidi was commissioned to restore the frescoes painted in the Vatican by the 16th-century Italian Renaissance master, Raphael. Following political upheavals in Rome, during which he was imprisoned and threatened with death, Brumidi left Italy and moved to America, arriving in New York in 1852. Three years later, he was commissioned to work on the U.S. Capitol building in Washington, D.C., and he labored at the project until his death in 1880. His painting *Cincinnatus at the Plough* hangs in the Agricultural

Constantino Brumidi's frescoes grace the walls of the U.S. Capitol.

In 1961 Elia Kazan (left) directed Natalie Wood and Warren Beatty in Splendor in the Grass.

Committee room in the Capitol. This work was the first in America to use the Italian technique, fresco (whereby paint is applied directly onto a moist plaster surface).

When Brumidi was 70, he began painting the Capitol's curved ceiling, the Rotunda. In spite of his advanced age, he worked on scaffolding suspended more than 100 feet from the ceiling, and for years curious visitors could gaze up at the striking figure of the old man with snow-white hair and beard as he hoisted himself by a system of pulleys to what he called his "shop." To many, Brumidi strongly resembled another great painter who worked in St. Peter's Cathedral in Rome, and for this reason he came to be known as the "Michelangelo of the U.S. Capitol."

One of many Greeks who immigrated from Turkey to the United States was Elia Kazan. Born in 1909, he arrived in this country in 1913 and studied at Williams College and Yale University. After graduating, he co-founded the famous Actors Studio in New York, which has trained some of the nation's finest actors, including the film stars Marlon Brando and Al Pacino. Kazan eventually became a celebrated theater and film director. He won Academy Awards for directing the films *Gentlemen's Agreement* (1947), which focused on ethnic prejudice and discrimination in an affluent Northeastern community, and *On the Waterfront* (1954), about dockworkers exploited by brutal racketeers.

Among Greek-American celebrities, Telly Savalas may be the most familiar to the American public. Born in New York in 1926, Savalas graduated from Columbia University, then worked for the federal government before becoming a professional actor, known for his nu-

Although best known as the star of the television series "Kojak," Telly Savalas has also written screenplays and directed films.

Greek-American diva Maria Callas moved to Athens at age 13 to study voice at the Royal Conservatory there.

merous performances as a "tough guy." His best-known role was as a Greek-American police detective in the popular television series "Kojak," which aired from 1973 to 1978. Savalas has retained a strong identification with his Greek roots, and every year on Greek Independence Day he can be seen on Fifth Avenue in New York City, heading a parade of jubilant Greek Americans.

Many other Greeks have also achieved renown in the arts. Dimitris Mitropoulos was born in Greece in 1896. As a boy he dreamed of becoming a Greek Orthodox monk until he learned that the religious order forbade the use of musical instruments. He then rejected the priesthood in favor of his true passion, the piano. Later he gravitated toward composing and conducting. After leading major European and American symphony orchestras, he became the principal conductor of the New York Philharmonic, a position he retained until his death in 1960.

Maria Callas (1923–1977), born in New York City but raised in Greece, eventually became one of opera's most celebrated voices of the 20th century, unsurpassed for her combination of vocal and dramatic gifts. Other notable artists include painter and sculptor Lucas Samaras (born in 1936), and actor and film director John Cassavetes (born in 1929), renowned for films such as *Gloria*, *A Woman Under the Influence*, and *Faces*.

Commerce

Greek immigrants had their greatest success in the United States as small entrepreneurs, but some of them eventually became giants of American industry. One such was Charles Maliotis. Born in Greece in 1895, he came to America as a 13 year old and roamed the streets of New York City, looking for a job. He eventually became a leading American industrialist and manufacturer of nuts, bolts, and similar hardware, and an important benefactor of the Greek-American community. Thomas Pappas (1898–1978) achieved prominence in the import-export food trade and became the director of the Exxon industrial complex in Greece.

An early case of Greek-American business success was a New York company that traded in cotton in the mid-1800s called Ralli Brothers. This firm was managed by Demetrios Botassi, a Greek diplomat stationed in the United States. By the 1850s, various businesses had been started by Greek immigrants in cities as diverse as New Orleans, Louisiana, and New York City.

More Greek Americans entered commerce at the turn of the 20th century. Spyros Skouras (1893–1971), one of the eleven children of a poor Greek farmer, arrived in New York City in 1912 wearing a suit he had bought with savings from a six-month job bailing hay and cleaning animal dung from the barns of well-to-do landlords. Failing to find a job in New York, he hopped

Spyros P. Skouras was a penniless 19 year old when he immigrated to the United States. Before long he had risen to the top of the movie industry.

a train to an unknown destination. The conductor kicked him off the next day, and Skouras found himself in St. Louis. He started working there as a waiter but soon saved enough money to enter the nickelodeon business—the ancestor of today's movie theater. Joined by two of his brothers, Skouras began purchasing theaters around the country and formed the Skouras theater chain. He became one of the most important figures in the industry and initiated some of its major innovations, such as "Cinemascope."

Spyros was the first man to let blacks into theaters in Missouri. Later, when he financed films of his own, he always deleted racial or ethnic slurs and insinuations. Eventually he reached the pinnacle of the film industry, becoming the president of 20th Century-Fox Film Corporation. During his tenure Spyros discovered or promoted so many stars—including Elizabeth Taylor, Marilyn Monroe, Tyrone Power, Henry Fonda, and Gregory Peck—that he came to be known as "the Greek Star-Maker." His power over the film industry was immense. At one time he controlled 20th Century-Fox, National Theaters, Fox West Coast Theaters, United Artists Theaters Circuit, Skouras Theaters, Magna Corporation, and Todd A-O, a degree of power attained by few other individuals in the film industry before or since.

For many years, corporate decision-making was the province of white Anglo-Saxon Protestants, the oldest immigrant group in North America and therefore the most entrenched. Their virtual monopoly over corporate management was reinforced by an "old-boy" network that kept top positions off limits to ethnic minorities. Some American-born sons of Greek immigrants, however, began to break through these walls guarded by tradition and elitism. Peter Peterson (born in 1926), originally Petropoulos, served as Secretary of

In 1978 37-year-old Paul Tsongas became the youngest member of the U.S. Senate when he won a Massachusetts seat.

In 1968, Republican vice-presidential nominee Spiro T. Agnew addresses a convention of the Veterans of Foreign Wars.

Commerce under Richard Nixon, U.S. president from 1968 to 1974. He subsequently became chairman of the board of the Blackstone Group, one of the largest investment banking firms in America. Another Greek American, William Tavoulareas (born in 1919), served as chairman of the board of the Mobil Oil Corporation.

Like business, American politics has traditionally been inaccessible to many ethnic groups. Race, religion, and even difficult-to-pronounce names often have proved insurmountable obstacles to minority members seeking elective office. Yet even during the early 19th century, when there were fewer than 2,000 Greek Americans in the entire country, the war orphan Lucas

Miller was elected to Congress. Still, he was an exception; most of the Greek Americans who attained major political offices emerged in the 1970s. Since then a number of politicians of Greek descent have played a role in the democratic process that originated nearly 2,500 years ago in Athens. Despite constituting no more than 0.2 percent of the nation's total population, Greek Americans are well represented in Congress, mostly as members of the Democratic Party.

Paul Sarbanes, born in 1933, the son of an immigrant café owner, graduated from Princeton, was a Rhodes Scholar, then received a law degree from Harvard. A Democratic representative from Maryland, he served on the House Judiciary Committee that probed the Watergate scandal of the Nixon era. He was elected to the Senate in 1976 and in 1987 took part in the Congressional panel investigating the Iran-Contra affair that occurred under President Ronald Reagan. Paul E. Tsongas, a Democratic senator from Massachusetts, was born in 1941. The son of an immigrant tailor, he graduated from Dartmouth and from Yale Law School and won his Senate seat in 1978. Other congressmen of Greek descent are Gus Yatron (born in 1927), Pennsylvania Democrat; Nicholas Mavroules (born in 1927), Massachusetts Democrat; L.A. "Skip" Bafalis (born in 1929), Florida Republican; and Olympia Bouchles Snowe (born in 1947), a Maine Republican who spent her childhood in the Greek Orthodox orphanage in Garrison, New York, and went on to become the youngest woman ever elected to the House in 1978. Other Greek Americans who held congressional seats in the 1970s include Peter N. Kyros (born in 1925), a Maine Democrat, and Nick Galifianakis (born in 1928), a Democrat from North Carolina.

At the local level, the Greeks who have been elected mayors of cities include George Christopher (born in 1907), San Francisco; Lee Alexander (born in 1927), Syracuse, New York; George Athanson, Hartford, Connecticut; Helen Boosalis (born in 1919), Lincoln, Nebraska; and John Roussakis (born in 1929), Savannah, Georgia.

Perhaps the best-known Greek-American politician has had the least illustrious career, though it began promisingly enough. Spiro T. Agnew was born in Baltimore, Maryland, in 1918. He attended local schools, then in 1949 entered the legal profession. Soon he gravitated toward politics, joining the Republican party, which helped him win election as Baltimore County's chief executive in 1961. Six years later he became governor of Maryland and in 1968 Republican presidential nominee Richard M. Nixon chose Agnew as his running-mate. After a hard-fought campaign, the Republican ticket won, and Agnew became America's 39th vice-president. A highly controversial figure, he questioned the loyalty of intellectuals and college students who opposed the Vietnam War and accused reporters in the press and on television of biased news coverage. A favorite among conservative Republicans, Agnew emerged as a potential presidential candidate, especially after he and Nixon won election to a second term in 1972. Then, as the Watergate scandal gripped Washington, the U.S. Justice Department uncovered evidence that Agnew had accepted bribes during his years in Maryland politics and that he had failed to pay federal taxes. Forced to resign the vice-presidency on October 10, 1973, Agnew eventually was fined $10,000 by a federal court and sentenced to three years' probation. Suddenly a man who had been a source of pride for Greek Americans became a source of embarrassment.

Many Greek Americans believe that Michael Dukakis, born in 1933 and elected governor of Massachusetts in 1974, will add luster to the story of Greek Americans in politics. The son of Greek immigrants, he was educated at Swarthmore College and received his law degree from Harvard. In 1962 he was elected to the Massachusetts House of Representatives and was elected Democratic governor of Massachusetts 12 years later. Dukakis lost the election in 1978 but won again

In April 1987 Massachusetts governor Michael Dukakis declared his presidential candidacy in Manchester, New Hampshire.

in 1982. A strong advocate of consumer rights, he was the first American legislator to introduce no-fault automobile insurance. He has transferred his own informal personal style (he uses public transportation daily) to his administration, where he has eliminated many of the trappings of his office, such as armed guards and chauffeured limousines. Dukakis holds frequent press conferences and open meetings with the people of Massachusetts. In 1988, with particularly strong support from the Greek-American community, he won the Democratic presidential nomination. ❧

In April 1967 members of a newly formed military junta gathered in Athens for their first official government meeting.

LOOKING AHEAD

The first Greek immigrants came to this country with very little education and almost no knowledge of the English language. Yet they overcame these obstacles with surprising ease and won a secure place in their adopted homeland. The group's desire for success found fertile ground in America, where they were allowed to struggle alongside other recent immigrants and to earn the respect of more privileged and established peoples.

The ancient Greek legacy of reason, resourcefulness, and adventurousness lives on in the vital presence this ethnic community continues to exert throughout the United States. In regions such as New England—specifically Boston, where as long ago as the early 19th century, wise leaders urged the population to focus on long-range achievements rather than short-term gains—Greek immigrants and their American-born offspring have made spectacular gains. Greek Americans now hold important positions in banking, law, and politics, as well as in business, education, and the arts.

Since World War II a new surge of Greek immigrants has landed on our shores. Like their forebears, these new arrivals have come mostly from rural backgrounds, and like them they have managed to make headway in the United States without sacrificing their unique heritage. This later group differs from the earlier immigrants, however, in one crucial respect: it includes a considerable number who brought highly developed professional skills to the New World, and also liberal attitudes. These distinctions have caused a rift in the Greek-American community.

The rift became apparent in 1967, when the historically harmonious relationship between the United States and Greece received a rude shock in consequence of turmoil in Greek politics. A military junta, or committee, seized power and established a dictatorship that strictly curtailed citizens' basic rights: freedom of the press, freedom of speech, and freedom of assembly. This meant that churches, political parties, social organizations, and trade unions could not exist.

The United States backed the military junta for seven years—from 1967 to 1974—and further acted against the interests of Greece by supporting Turkey when its troops invaded the island of Cyprus (an independent republic composed of Greek and Turkish people), occupied Greek lands and business establishments and turned thousands of Greek Cypriots into refugees.

The conflicts between the U.S. and Greek governments divided the Greek-American community, the

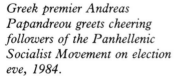

Greek premier Andreas Papandreou greets cheering followers of the Panhellenic Socialist Movement on election eve, 1984.

majority of whom sided with the military regime in Greece. The most apparent explanation for their attitude is that by 1967, Greek Americans had, on the whole, become so prosperous in their new land that they chose not to question the policies of the United States. It may also be that as Greek Americans grew more conservative they lost touch with the hardships suffered by those still living in the old country.

In any case, not all Greek Americans shared this view. The newer immigrants—the well-educated professionals—objected to the military regime and also to the attitudes of the older Greek Americans, whom they accused of being complacent and self-satisfied, and of having lost sight of their community's best interests. Such discord is a familiar story in America, where each generation feels the need to break free of established habits and introduce fresh ideas.

Greek Americans, though, have a better chance of mending their differences than many of their compatriots. After all, they are the inheritors of the glorious tradition that taught the Western world the importance of reason and debate and rational persuasion. It is now up to Greek Americans to wield these ancient skills for the purpose of uniting their own diverse community.

Turkish paratroopers display their nation's flag after landing in Nicosia, Cyprus, on July 20, 1974.

FURTHER READING

Bowra, C. M. *The Greek Experience*. New York: New American Library, 1957.

Burgess, Thomas. *Greeks in America*. Boston: Sherman, French & Co., 1913.

Cutsumbis, Michael. *A Bibliographic Guide to Greeks in the United States, 1850–1968*. New York: Center for Migration Studies, 1970.

Fairchild, Henry Platt. *Greek Immigrants to the United States*. New Haven: Yale University Press, 1911.

Hooper, Finley. *Greek Realities: Life and Thought in Ancient Greece*. Detroit: Wayne State University Press, 1978.

Leber, George T. *The History of the AHEPA, 1922–1972, Including the Greeks in the New World and Immigrants to the United States*. Washington, DC: The Order of AHEPA, 1972.

Monos, Dimitris. *The Achievements of the Greeks in the United States*. Philadelphia: Centrum Scientific and Scholarly Publications, 1986.

Saloutos, Theodore. *The Greeks in the United States*. Cambridge: Harvard University Press, 1964.

Zotos, Stephanos. *Hellenic Presence in America*. Wheaton, IL: Pilgrimage, 1967.

INDEX

"Philhellenes," 38–40
Philip II, 29
Philosophy, 24–25, 28–29, 31, 34, 91
Piraeus, 35
Pius IX, Pope, 91
Plato, 24, 28–29
Plato Society, 74, 88
Poland, 34
Protestant church, 31, 49, 64, 97

Quincy, Josiah, 38

Raphael, 91
Reagan, Ronald, 99
Reconstruction, 46
Refugee Relief Act, 14
Religious freedom, 30
Renaissance, 34, 91
Republican party, 99–101
Republic, The (Plato), 24–25
Rhode Island, 51
Roman Catholic church, 31–33
Roman Empire, 29–32
Romania, 14
Rome, Italy, 29–31, 78, 91
Russia, 34, 77

Saloutos, Theodore, 61
Samaras, Lucas, 95
Savalas, Telly, 93
Schliemann, Heinrich, 21
Science, 29, 34, 87, 90
Senate, U.S., 99
"Seven Wisemen," 23
Sicily, 21
Skouras, Spyros, 95–97
Slavs, 32
Socrates, 24, 28
Solon, 22–23
Sophocles, 24
Soviet Union, 77. See also Russia

Spain, 21, 37
Sparta, 24, 27, 73
Strickland, William, 42
Sweden, 49

Tavoulareas, William, 98
Theater. See Drama
Theseus, 75
Thrace, 73
Thucydides, 28
Trojan War, 21
Troy, 19, 20–21
Turkey, 14, 21, 33–34, 39, 40, 62, 64, 78, 93, 104. See also Asia Minor

Unemployment, 46, 82
United Nations, 77
United States census, 14, 82
U.S. Immigration and Naturalization Service, 13–14
Utah, 45, 52

Valeriano, Apostolo. See De Fuca, Juan
Vasarras, 88
Vatican, 31, 91
Venice, Italy, 32, 34, 78
Verenthi, 88
Vietnam War, 100

War of Independence, 42, 62
Warsaw Pact, 77
Washington, D.C., 75, 91–92, 100
Watergate, 99–100
Webster, Daniel, 38
World War I, 77, 85
World War II, 14–15, 55, 77, 103

Yatron, Gus, 99

Zachos, John Celivergeos, 39–40
Zeus, 28

PICTURE CREDITS

We would like to thank the following sources for providing photographs: American School of Classical Studies: p. 20; AP/Wide World Photos: pp. 86–87, 96, 97, 98, 101, 102–103, 104, 105; Alinari/Art Resource: pp. 16, 26, 31, 65: Giraudon/Art Resource: pp. 18, 39; Marburg/Art Resource: p. 25; Balch Institute for Ethnic Studies: cover, pp. 62, 78, 83; The Bettmann Archive: pp. 36–37, 38, 76–77, 92, 94; The British Museum: p. 30; Thomas Doulis: pp. 48–49, 51, 56; German Archaeological Institute of Athens: p. 19; Hirmer Photoarchive: p. 33; Institute of Texan Cultures: pp. 35, 54; Andrew T. Kopan: pp. 57, 60, 73, 80; Library of Congress: pp. 52, 91; The Metropolitan Museum of Art: p. 22; Museum of American Textile History: p. 47; National Archives: pp. 12–13; National Library of Medicine: pp. 88, 89; Nebraska Historical Society: p. 50; New York Public Library: pp. 40, 41, 84; Reuters/Bettmann Newsphotos: p. 93; Mark Stein Studios: pp. 28, 32; Katrina Thomas: pp. 53, 61, 66–72, 74; United Nations: p. 23; University of Illinois at Chicago, Jane Addams Memorial Collection: p. 44; UPI/Bettmann Newsphotos: pp. 15, 43; Utah State Historical Society: pp. 58–59.

DIMITRIS MONOS was born in Greece and received his high school education in Athens, then came to the United States. He has taught at the University of Pennsylvania and at Georgetown University and is currently Associate Professor of Sociology and Director of the Institute for Ethnic Studies at West Chester University in West Chester, Pennsylvania. He is the author of *The Achievements of the Greeks in the United States*.

DANIEL PATRICK MOYNIHAN is the senior United States senator from New York. He is also the only person in American history to serve in the cabinets or subcabinets of four successive presidents—Kennedy, Johnson, Nixon, and Ford. Formerly a professor of government at Harvard University, he has written and edited many books, including *Beyond the Melting Pot, Ethnicity: Theory and Experience* (both with Nathan Glazer), *Loyalties,* and *Family and Nation*.